KU-008-178

BALLY
SINCE 1851

SKIRA

THE LIBRARY
WITHDRAWN
NEW COLLEGE
SWINDON

Project and text by
Moreno Gentili

Photographs by
Franco Garlaschelli

Art Director
Marcello Francone

Editorial Coordination
Giovanna Rocchi

Design and layout
Paola Ranzini

Editing
Charles Gute, Studio Carotti, Milano

Translations
Barbara Cooper, Language Consulting Congressi srl,
Milano

In collaboration with
Thomas Lenthal

First published in Italy in 2007 by
Skira Editore S.p.A.
Palazzo Casati Stampa
via Torino 61
20123 Milano
Italy
www.skira.net

© Bally Group 2007
© Peter Kopp, Niklaus Stoecklin,
Bernard Villemot by SIAE 2007
© 2007 The authors for their texts
© 2007 Franco Garlaschelli for his photographs
© 2007 Skira editor 2011001758

All rights reserved under international copyright
conventions.
No part of this book may be reproduced or utilized in
any form or by any means, electronic or mechanical,
including photocopying, recording, or any information
storage and retrieval system, without permission in
writing from the publisher.

Printed and bound in Italy. First edition

ISBN-13: 978-88-7624-873-3
ISBN-10: 88-7624-873-0

Distributed in North America by Rizzoli International
Publications, Inc., 300 Park Avenue South, New York,
NY 10010.
Distributed elsewhere in the world by Thames and
Hudson Ltd., 181A High Holborn, London WC1V 7QX,
United Kingdom.

I always had a passion for shoes. As a child, I would stand with my heels on the curb and my toes in the gutter, in an attempt to simulate the effect of high heels. When I was thirteen years old, my mother finally took me to Bally, and bought me my first pair of grown-up shoes—patent leather with Audrey Hepburn heels. I was giddy with delight."

I was excited to be asked by Bally to explore their extensive archive—to discover the wonders of the company's long heritage and history and, perhaps more importantly, the gorgeousness of their designs.

Shoes offer a strange dichotomy.

On one hand (or should that be foot?), they are born out of necessity, something we need every day: practical, worthy and duty-bound. On the other, they can be the stuff of dreams, objects of desire that offer us an elusive glimpse of fantasy.

Favourite fairy tales are full of extraordinary shoes: Cinderella had her exquisite slippers while Dorothy in the *Wizard of Oz* wore sparkling ruby courts. In the folktale of *Puss In Boots*, even the eponymous feline hero wears luxurious thigh-length leather boots. Shoes can inspire madness too. In the wildest moments of the Jazz Age suitors showed the depths of their desire by drinking champagne from the shoes of their paramours.

Today, shoes still have the power to provide a touch of glamour. Inherently sensual, who can resist the corseting of an ankle by fine leather straps or the sprinkling of rhinestones outlining a heel or sole.

There is a uniquely languid elegance about a two-tone brogue...a kinky eroticism in a strappy peep-toe. But the real magic of a truly fabulous pair of shoes is that they can provide more than we might wish for and take us to places we've never been before...

Iain R. Webb

The Age of Bally

At a certain point during his evolution, Man felt compelled toward new goals and aspirations. Foot coverings came into general use as soon as people began to travel farther in order to fulfil their dreams of conquest. And from then on, when Man discovered the vastness of the world around him, he chose to venture into it wearing things to protect him. Footwear was part of this lifestyle choice. It was not, however, until the Ancient Egyptians that the first notion of elegance, of wearing a shoe for its beauty, emerged. Shoe design was born.

Today we are here among the pages of this book to tell a story that began in 1851, when the industrialist Carl Franz Bally founded what was to become the first truly global luxury brand. This is the story of Bally, a company that has always united tradition and innovation, and continues to do so with unwavering skill in its quest to help people walk with comfort, elegance and style. It is a story that highlights the importance of footwear, or shoes, to the evolution of a civilization. And in case that were not enough – this model of both craftsmanship and industry, tradition and innovation, that produced footwear chosen by several million people over the course of two centuries – we should remember how much importance is attributed to this 'object' that provides comfort and style around the globe.

Everything actually began a little earlier, in 1847, when Carl Franz Bally and his brother took over an elastic tape and braces factory, a business started by their father. But the event that triggered footwear production was a token of love; or rather, a few pairs of low-cut decorated *bottines* that Carl Franz bought for his wife on a trip to Paris. This romantic story has a familiar cast: Carl's wife had asked for shoes, but having forgotten her size, he had to buy a dozen pairs in all sizes and designs. All of the variations in qual-

The Bally factory in full swing. Schönenwerd, Switzerland, 1888

ity of materials, sizes, styles and price-points gave him a vision of shoes for every type of person and every type of situation, whether going to a ball or hiking in the mountains. He realized it was his calling to bring industrialization to Switzerland. When he got back to his hometown and saw the enormous enthusiasm the shoes provoked he immediately launched the production of the first Bally shoes.

The first few years were full of adversity. Working with the existing business, they attempted to make the first shoes out of elastic. This did not work; his employees were not skilled at shoe making and had no desire to learn the trade. The banks thought he was crazy and would not back him, and other small shoe businesses, threatened by the competition, were antagonistic. Despite this early adversity and some small failures, he did not lose his enthusiasm and belief in his project. He gathered together knowledgeable professionals from all over Europe and started production that soon became enormously successful.

At the beginning the shoes were still handmade. But what was interesting from an industrial point of view was the way the work was organized. His employees were treated with complete respect. The first factory was actually just a house, with 30 skilled craftsmen, 30 beds, sewing machines and weaving looms. To the modern reader this does not sound appealing, but these workers, mostly women, got along so well it was reported that they sang and sometimes even danced while they worked. As a modern industrialist Carl Franz had many farsighted ideas, and he was open to his employees' input. Notably, there were little drawers on the premises he called 'New Idea' drawers; any employee was welcome to submit suggestions on how to improve working conditions or the business in general. The best ideas were rewarded with a cash prize and a diploma, a wonderful and original incentive scheme.

Bally's first London store, crowded with customers.
London, early 20th century

An employee cutting a shoe model from a
sheet of leather in Bally's Schönenwerd plant
in Switzerland, 1947

Carl's son Eduard was in charge of research, travelling to the US and to England in search of technologies to adapt for their purposes. Production was really launched in 1854 when the firm C.F.Bally was established and Bally's first shops opened in Berne, Basel and Zurich. Bally later introduced innovative machines of proprietary design, which sped up footwear production without altering the product's basic quality. Before the introduction of production machinery, a skilled shoemaker took 24 hours to make one pair of shoes. Bally's new equipment could produce over 100 pairs of shoes per day. At all times the Bally family were careful to make sure that the adoption of these new machines did not undermine the company's traditional values of craftsmanship, high quality, comfort and style.

By 1860 the company had 500 employees. The introduction of steam power and new machinery gave a huge boost to production. Schönenwerd soon acquired the characteristics of a company town, with Bally's progress paving the way for worker housing, schools, libraries and Schönenwerd's public park with swimming pools and public baths. All of this was thanks to Carl Franz's son Arthur, who was responsible for creating these social institutions that looked after the worker's well being; he even introduced medical insurance and pension plans.

Production became fully mechanized in 1870, enabling the company to expand into new markets. New branches in Montevideo, Buenos Aires, Paris and Geneva showcased new styles that were far more comfortable to wear and were in keeping with the fashions of the day. Despite being industrially made, the quality of the leather and design were typical of handmade footwear; Bally shoes soon became a byword for luxury.

Soon the company grew even further; its products became available in Alexandria, Barcelona, Beirut, Brussels, Bucharest, Cairo, Constantinople, Hamburg, Lisbon, Madrid

An employee sewing a shoe upper in Bally's Schönenwerd plant in Switzerland, 1948

Bally's Paris store, 1951

Marseilles, Sofia and Vienna. Bally's success reached even greater heights in 1892 when the firm founded its UK retail branch. The 'London Shoe Company' debuted with locations on New Bond, Victoria and Sloane Street, London's most famous shopping districts. This company only dealt with the finest luxury shoes of highest quality and design, something unprecedented at that time. The Royal family, members of the Royal household and high society all shopped there. From overseas and around the world people ordered shoes by mail from these stores. Eventually even Hollywood stars would become loyal customers, including Charlie Chaplin. In the same year that the London Shoe Company opened, Carl Franz – known to everyone as 'Papa' Bally – handed over the company to his sons. It was a record year, with two million pairs of shoes sold.

Industrial progress led to new machinery, while hand-worked materials and ornamentation continued Bally's tradition of fine craftsmanship. The early years of the 20th century were marked by new prosperity due to emerging markets in France, Italy, Germany and Austria. In those days, in order to bolster its fast-growing expansion, Bally began using illustrated posters as a form of advertising. These stylish posters were created by the best illustrators of the era, many from a Swiss school founded by Ferdinand Hodler, who developed a style called Parallelism and whose work graces the back of the 50-franc Swiss note.

The first Bally poster appeared in 1910, marking the start of a period of intense creativity. Renowned artists like Laubi, Baumberger, Berset and Villemot succeeded in making Bally's public image an ongoing legacy. This new approach to art and advertising was largely pioneered by Bally. Much of the original artwork created for Bally is today held in public and private collections around the world.

Bally's London store in the 1960s
Photo by Edgar Hyman

A new production record was set in 1916: some 3.9 million pairs of shoes were sold thanks not least to the firm's 7500 employees. During the Depression, Bally not only survived but also managed to set up a holding company with five sales divisions. The postwar boom enabled new factories to be built in Switzerland in the 1950s. Further modernized production lines opened the way to new export markets: South Africa, Belgium and Argentina.

During these years of great international expansion Bally enjoyed a number of major successes. Bally's research and development team worked closely with the United Nations to help companies set up production facilities in emerging nations; Bally's production-line organization skills, its standards for precision production and quality were a model for promoting a new manner of living around the world. Bally's hiking boots were worn by Sir Edmond Hillary's team on his first ever climb of Mount Everest. Bally even made the rubber components for the boots worn by Neil Armstrong during the first walk on the moon.

The Far-East market grew strongly in the 1980s. Bally Hong Kong, Bally Singapore and Bally Australia were founded. New stores opened in China, Saudi Arabia, Lebanon, Kuala Lumpur, Brazil, Columbia and Nepal. Since the 1800s Bally has maintained its global presence. Today there are currently some 200 dedicated Bally stores and over 600 points-of-sale worldwide.

One of the most important footwear manuals, still used around the world for teaching the art of shoemaking, is *L'Universe de la Chaussure* (Max Blattner, 2001). The standards set forth in this book are the fruit of Bally's years of experience and continual research.

A brand that has few equals in the world for its heritage and innovation, Bally has a

rich archive of all the styles created since its beginning – a resource that it still draws on for inspiration today. This book is a tribute to these shoes that in the collective imagination represent periods we look back upon with more than a little nostalgia.

An innovative eye for detail has always been Bally's hallmark throughout history. Brogueing and ribbon details actually did carryover from the elastic ribbon side of the business. Bally became famous for perfecting the use of *mignon* straps. The delicate use of these straps as a beautiful adornment for the foot was a difficult skill to master. Intricate stitching and two-tone colouring were also Bally trademarks. Shoe design at Bally blended the old and new, always loyal to the fundamental principle of 'tradition and innovation' that was, and still is, clear to customers around the world. These models epitomize a style based on elegance and comfort.

They say the shoe makes the outfit. It is true that a less-than-perfect outfit can be saved by the perfect pair of shoes, yet a perfect outfit can be ruined by bad shoes. In one form or other, in almost every culture, first impressions are often based on a quick glance at another person's feet. Bally, for over 155 years, has helped people across the world express their personalities and fulfil their desires.

"The journey of a thousand miles begins with a single step."

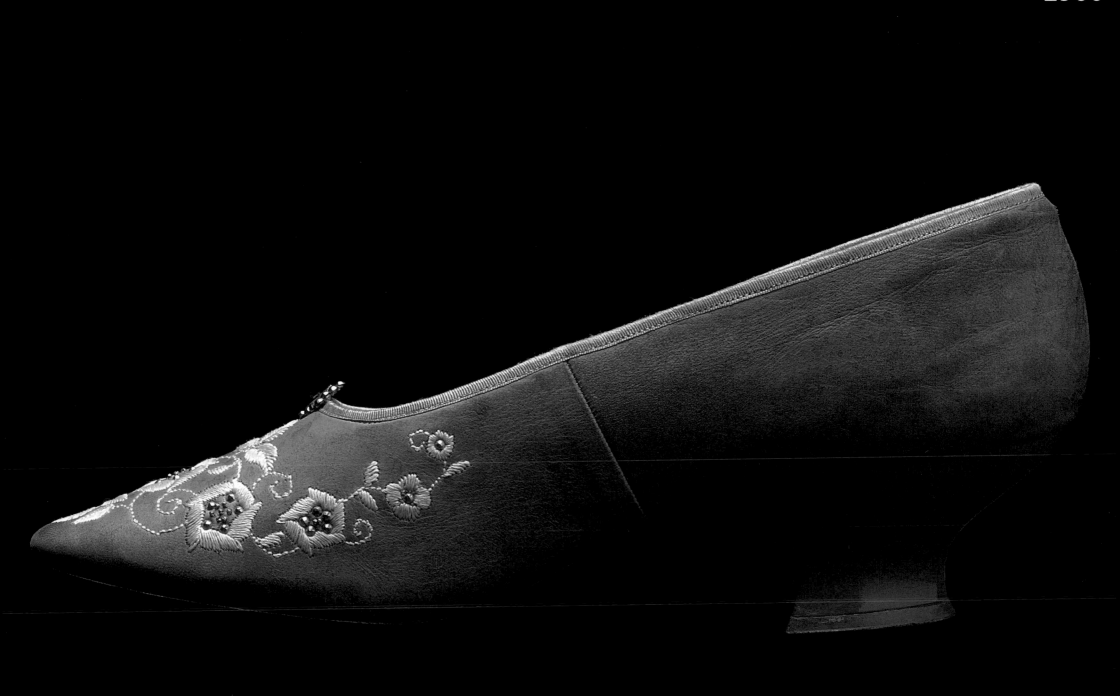

1915

„Bally's

FAMOUS
FOOTWEAR

32

Please send me your last pair of shoes, already worn out with dancing...
so that I might have something to press against my heart."

Goethe

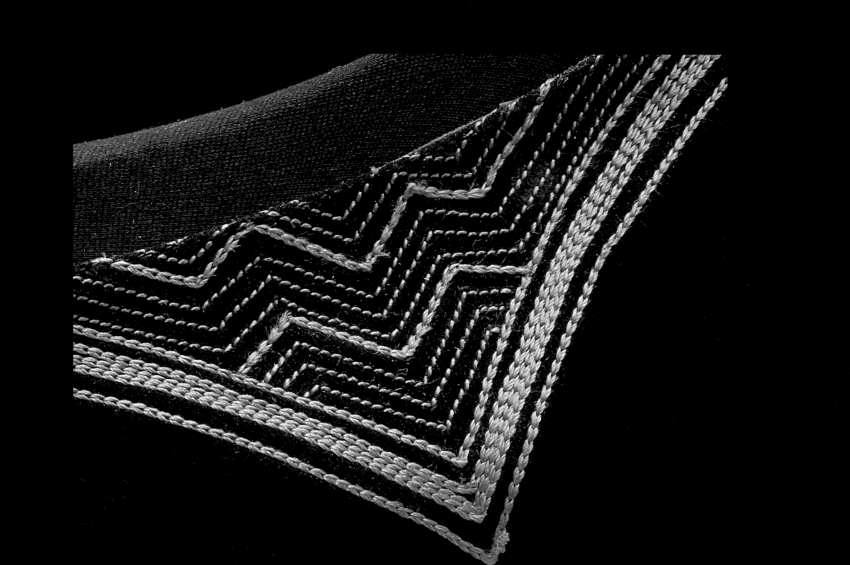

1922

1922

1925

I remember sitting in detention sophomore year with this really cute girl, and I remember asking her what she liked about certain guys. She said the first thing she looked at was a guy's shoes. That statement changed my life forever. Back then it was all about having clean gym shoes; that's why black guys always have white shoes. Having a new pair of shoes basically told the girl, 'I have a job and I can afford to take you

1926

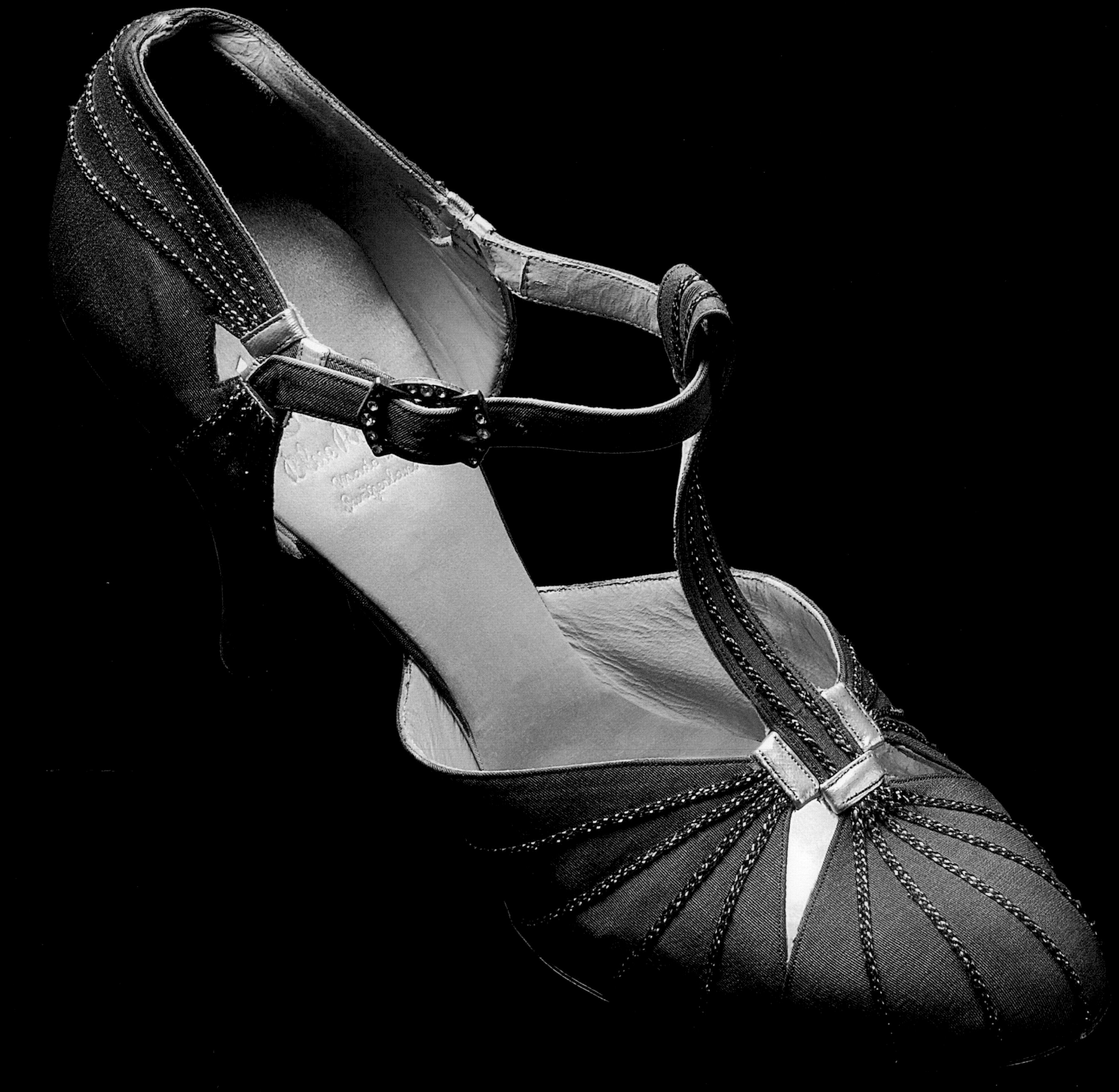

1926

Bally's

FINE SHOES

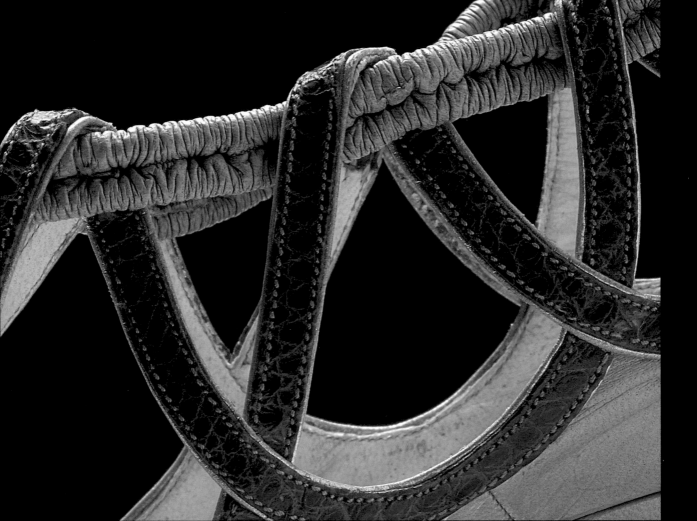

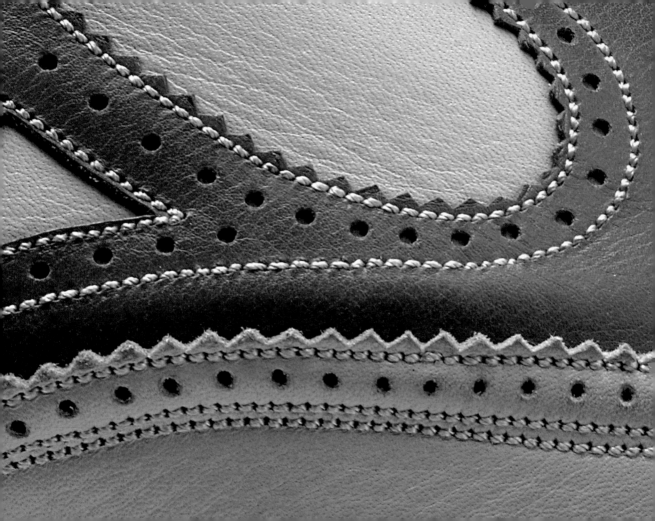

Bally

La grande Vogue

"Our ability to accessorize is what separates us from the animals."

Clairee Belcher, Steel Magnolias

1933

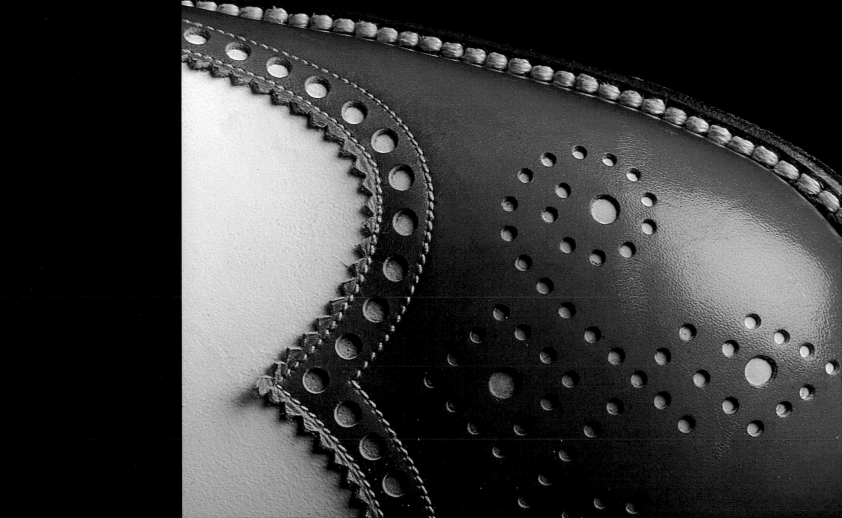

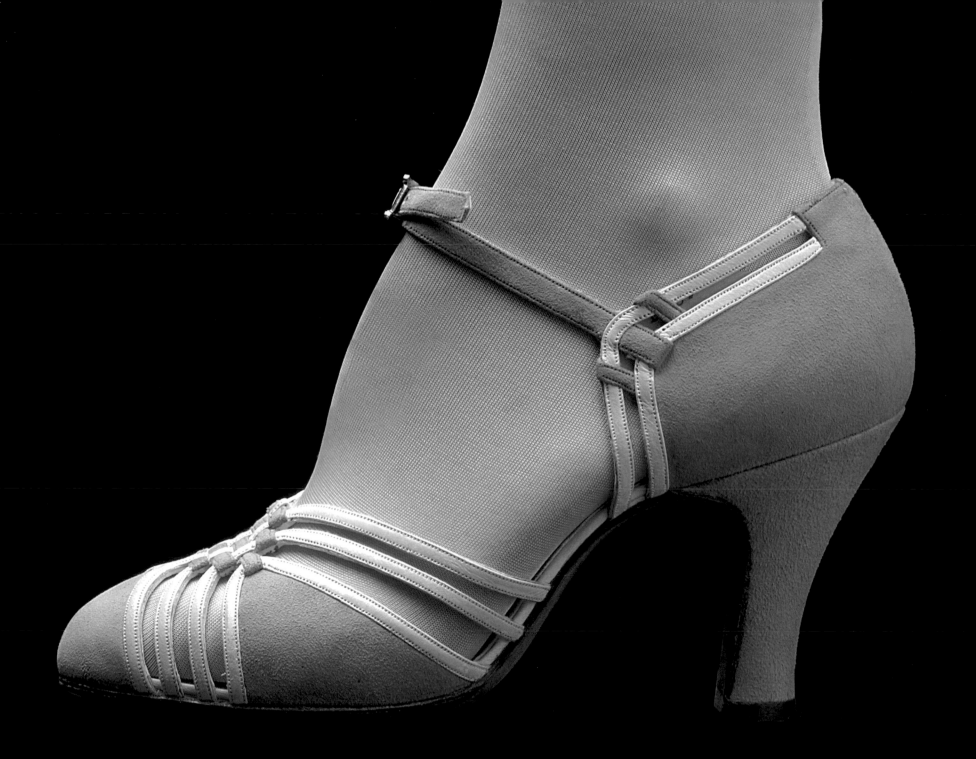

1935

"Give a girl the correct footwear and she can conquer the world."

Bette Midler

1937

1937

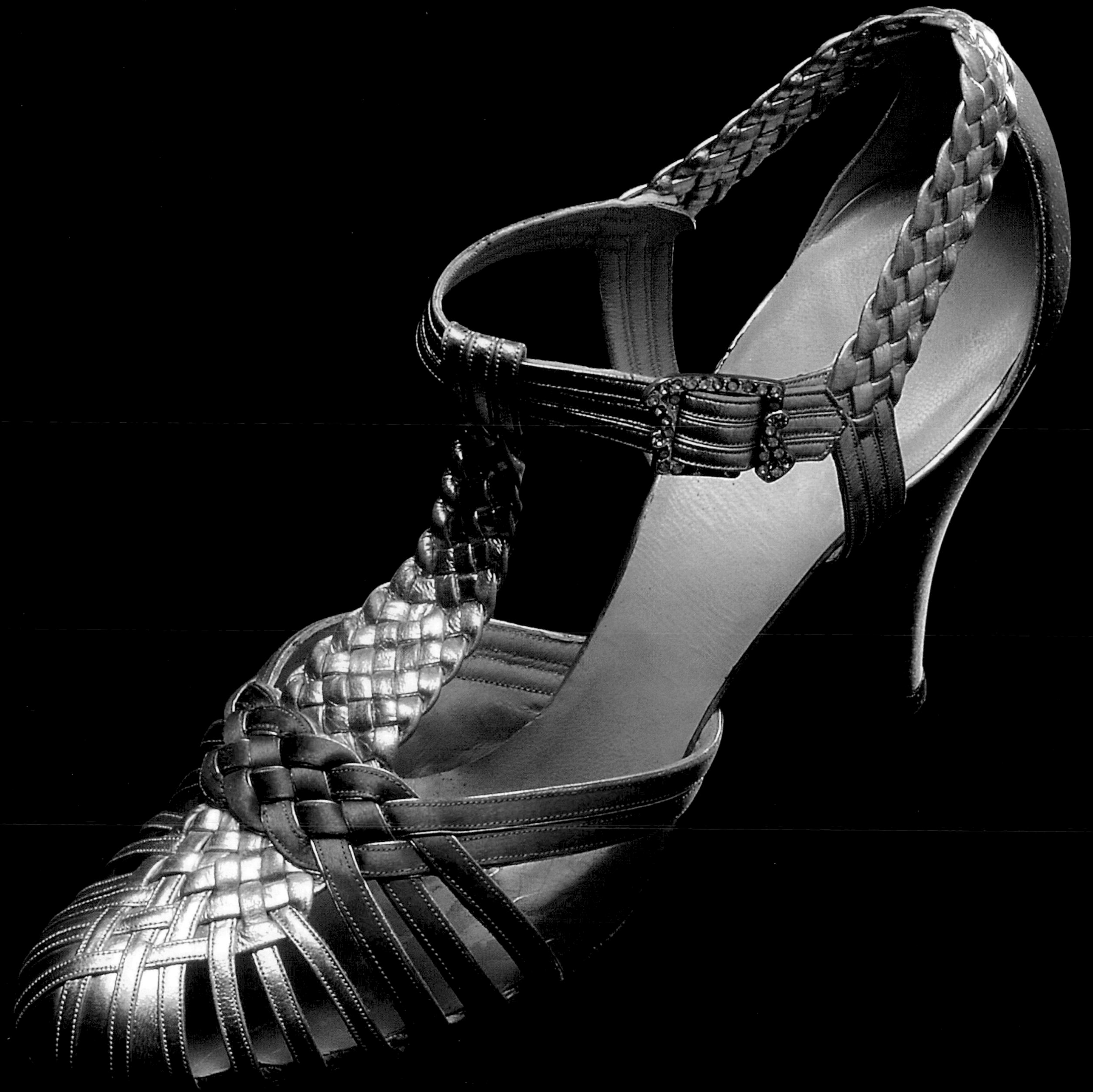

1938

Bally
CONFORT ELEGANCE QUALITE

1938

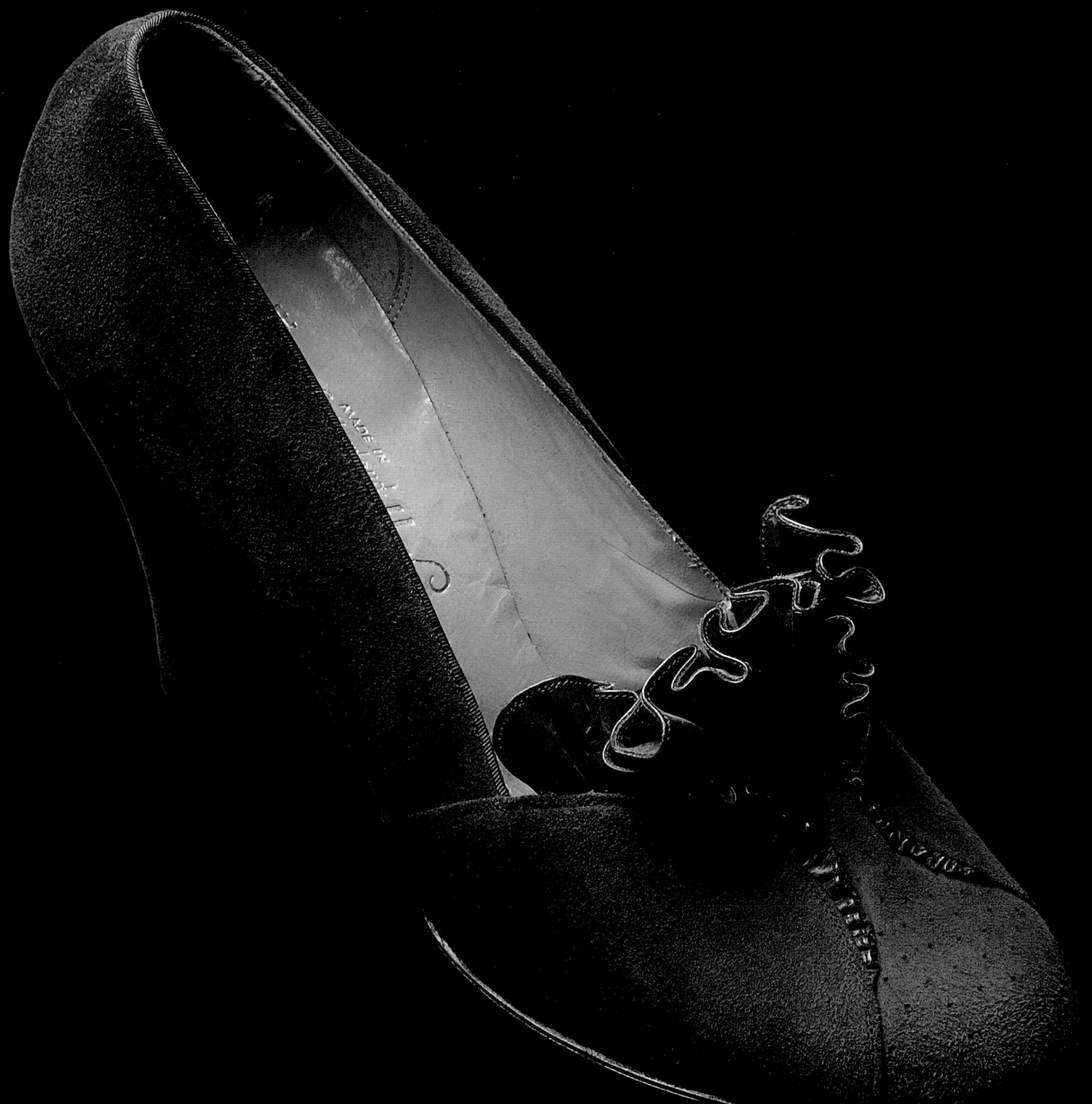

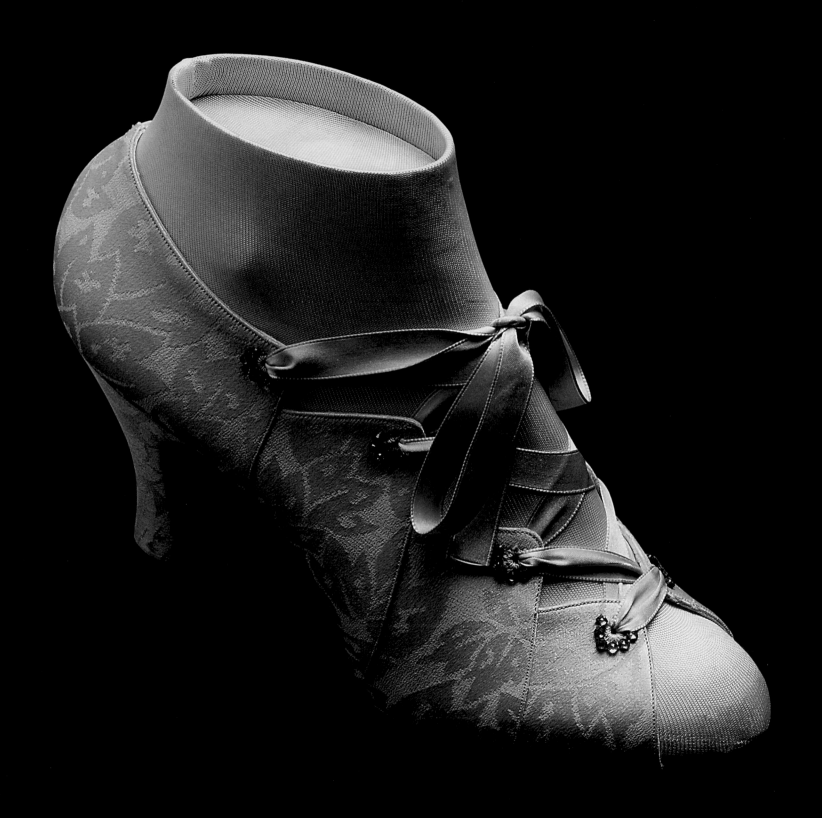

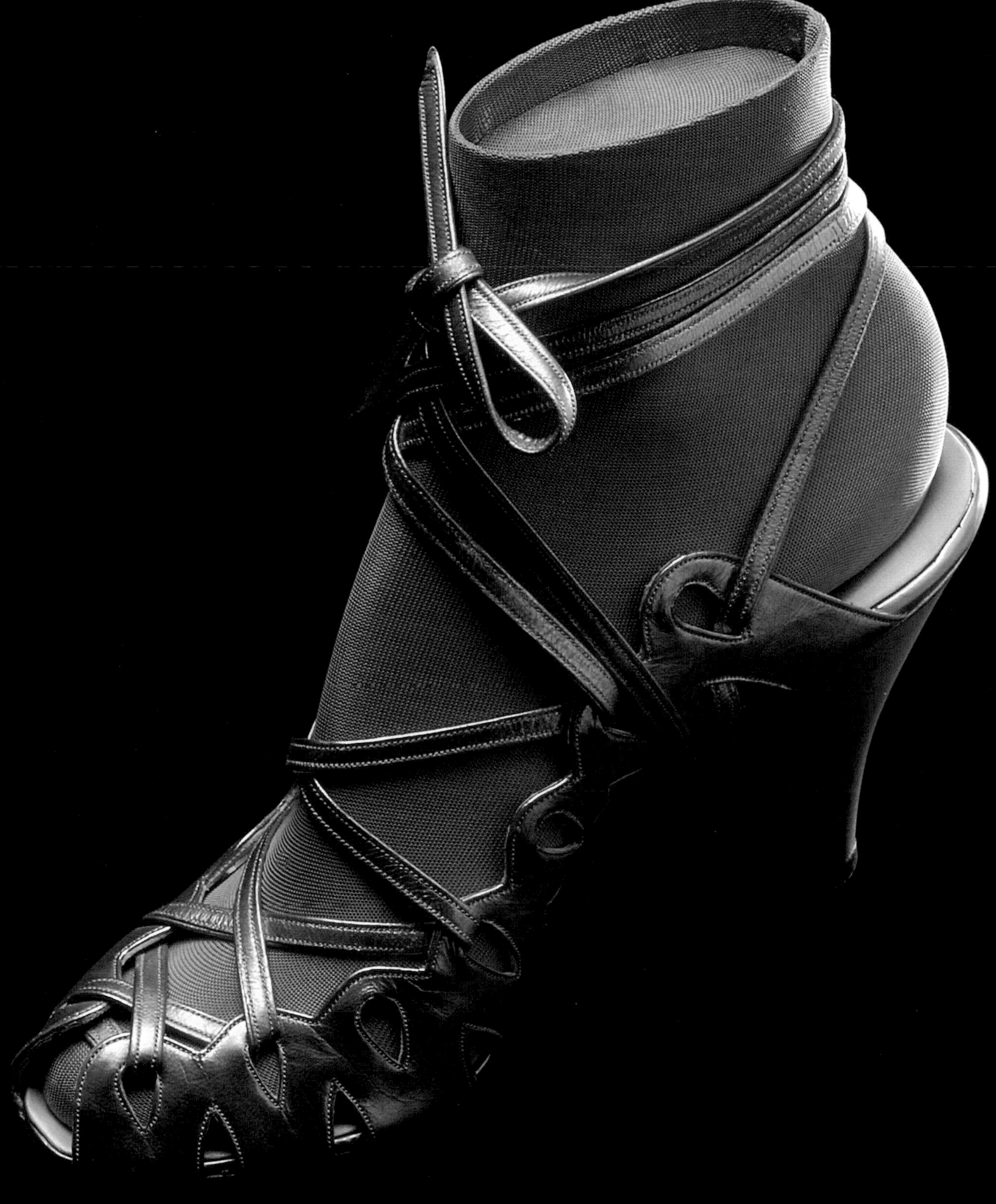

1939

"They say that clothes make the man; I say shoes make the woman. There is nothing that makes me feel more confident and feminine than a beautiful pair of shoes. Learning to walk in heels is a passage to womanhood. A fabulous shoe is like a piece of art or incredible architecture—they just demand to be appreciated."

Jessica Alba

1939

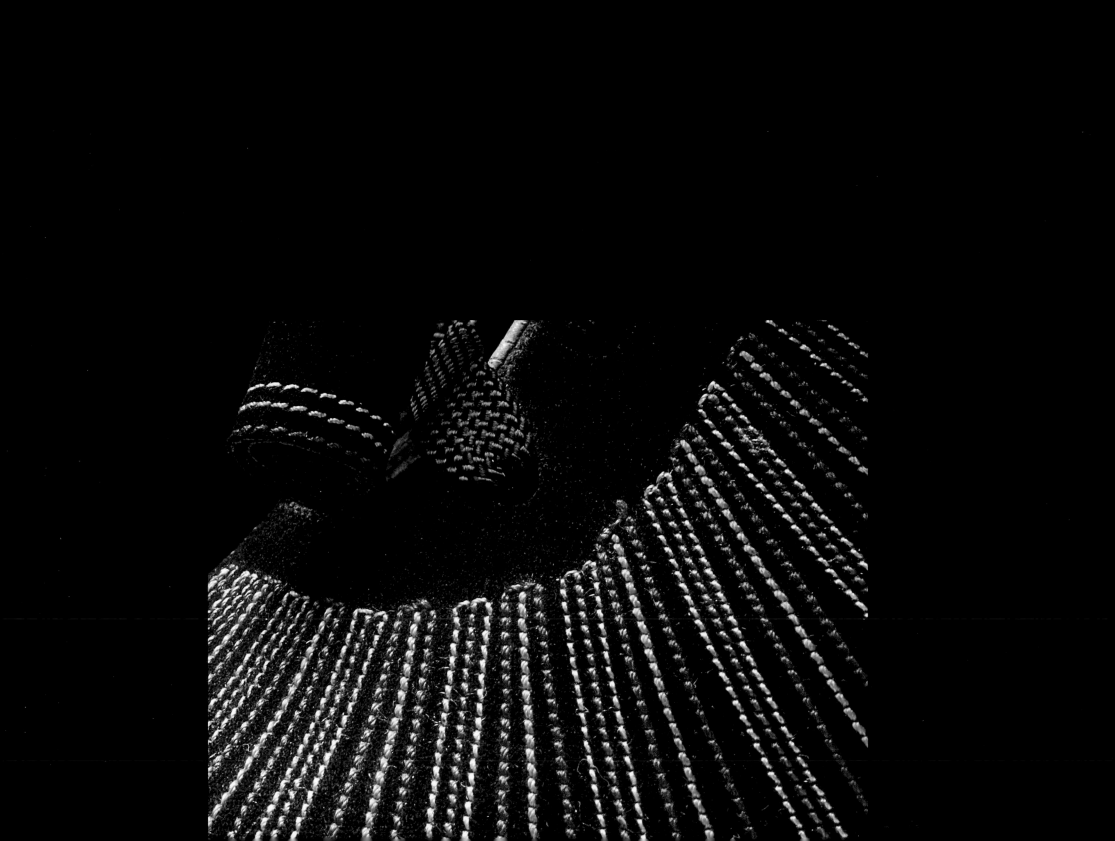

1939

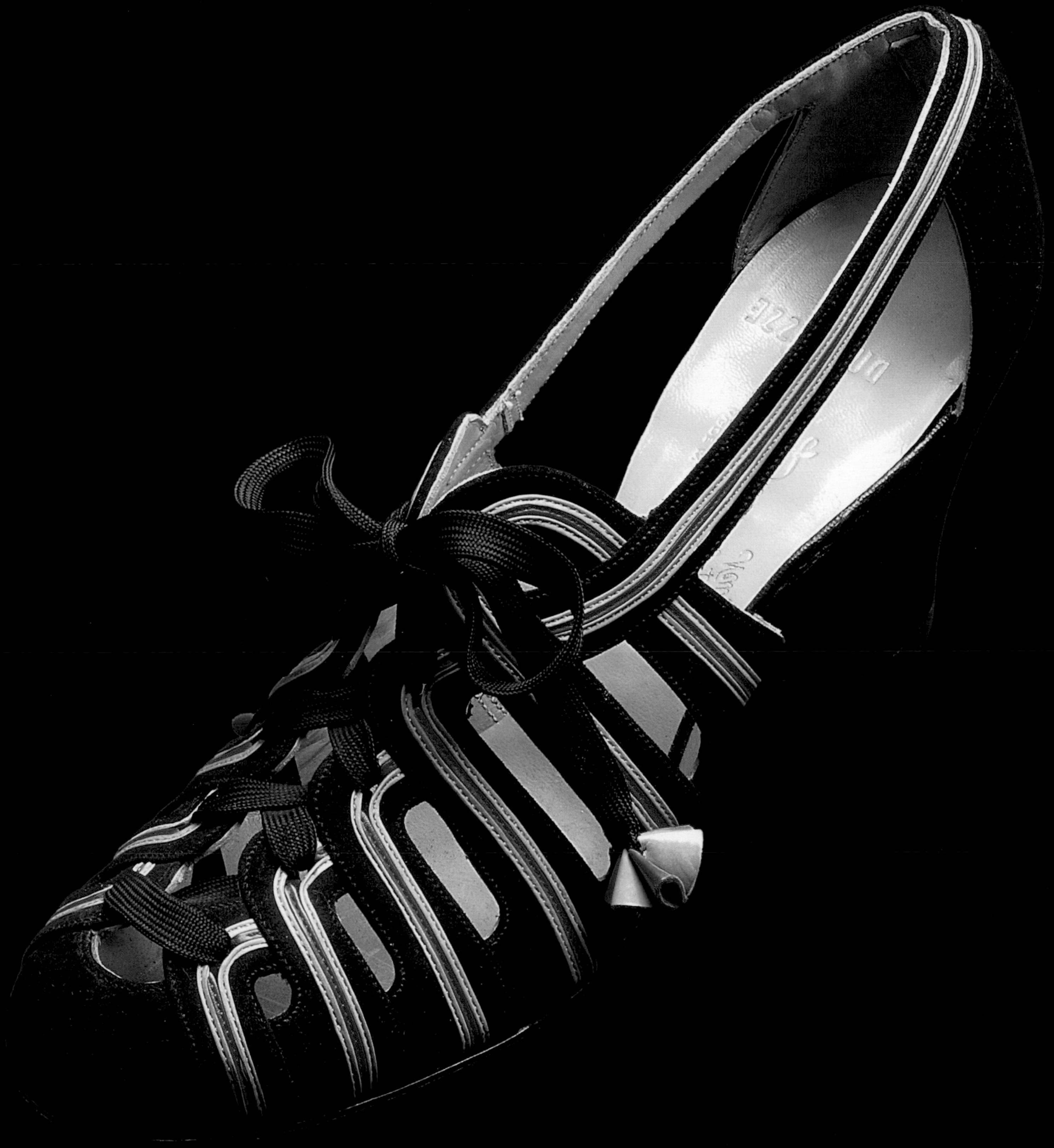

BALLY

PIERRE AUGSBURGER

"Mama always said there's an awful lot you can tell about a person by their shoes: where they're going, where they've been."

Forrest Gump

BALLY

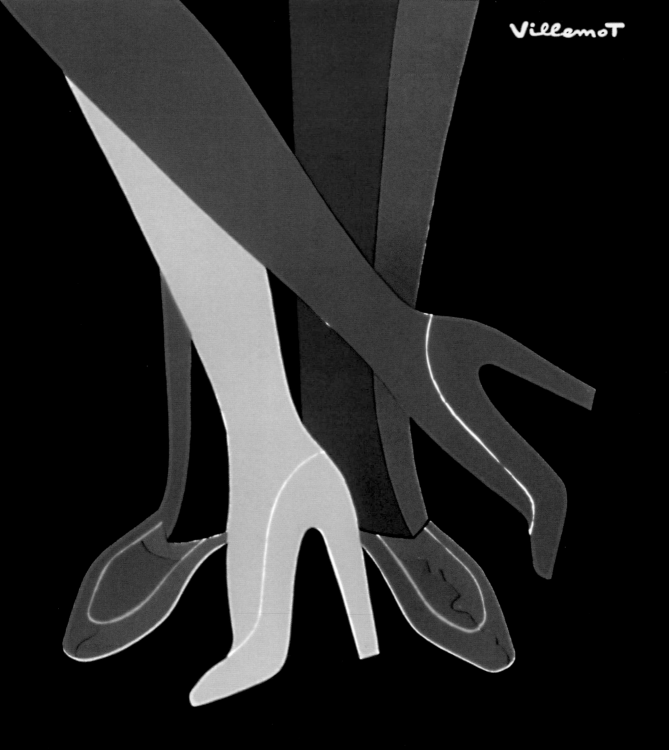

"I do not know who designed high heels, but all women owe him a lot."

Marilyn Monroe

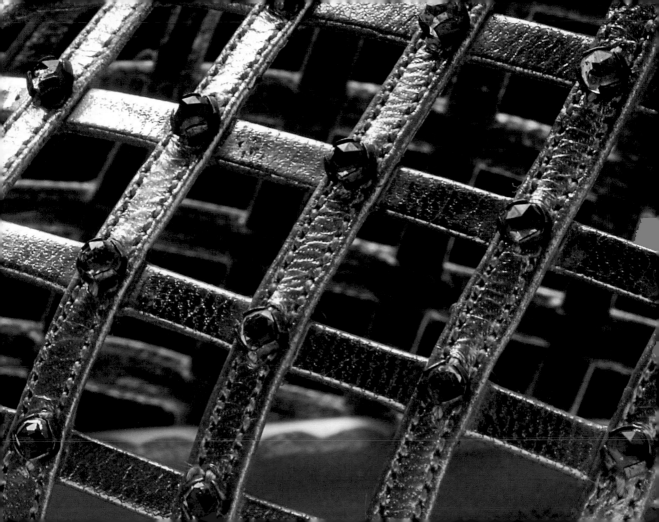

1951

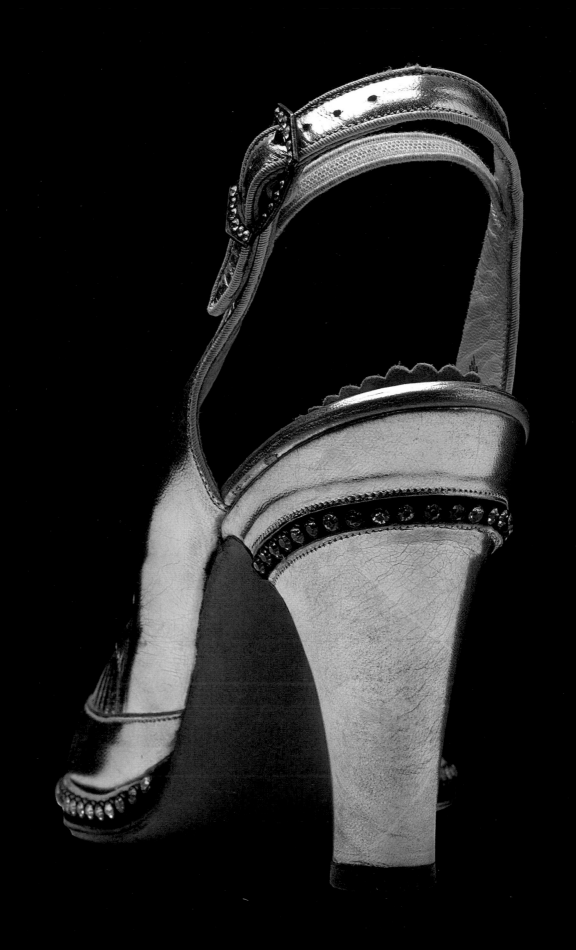

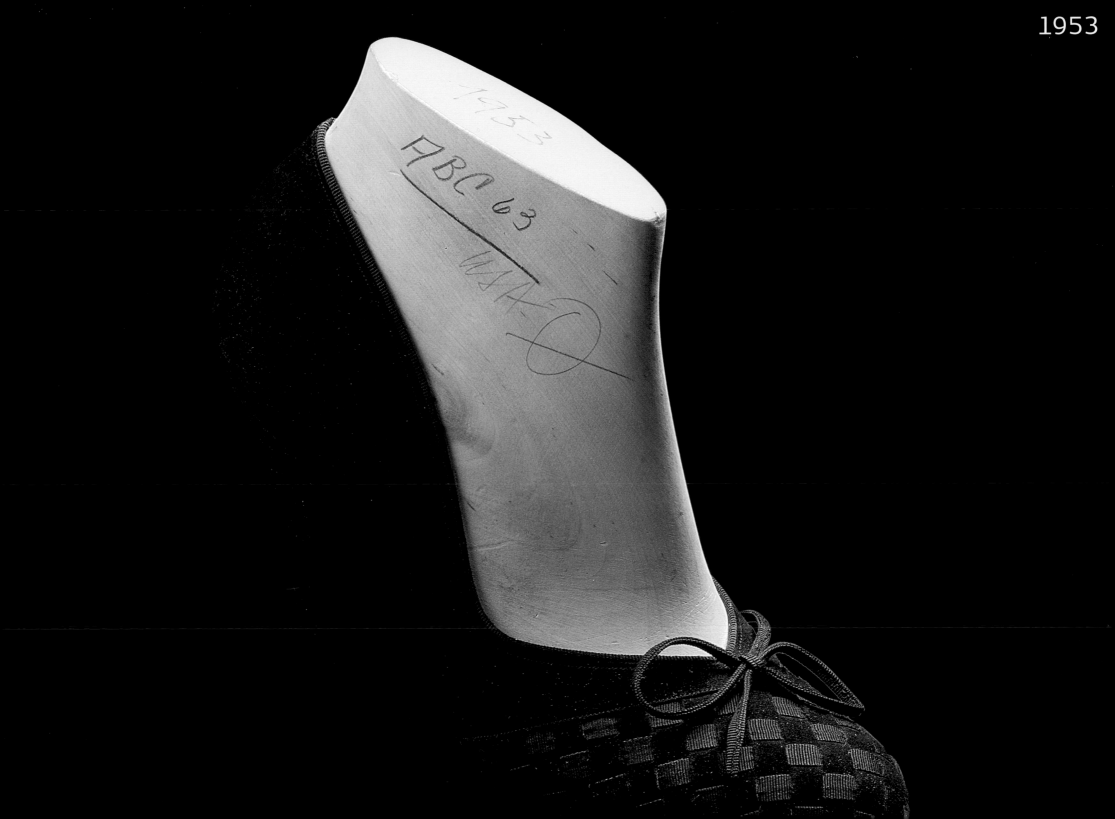

1954

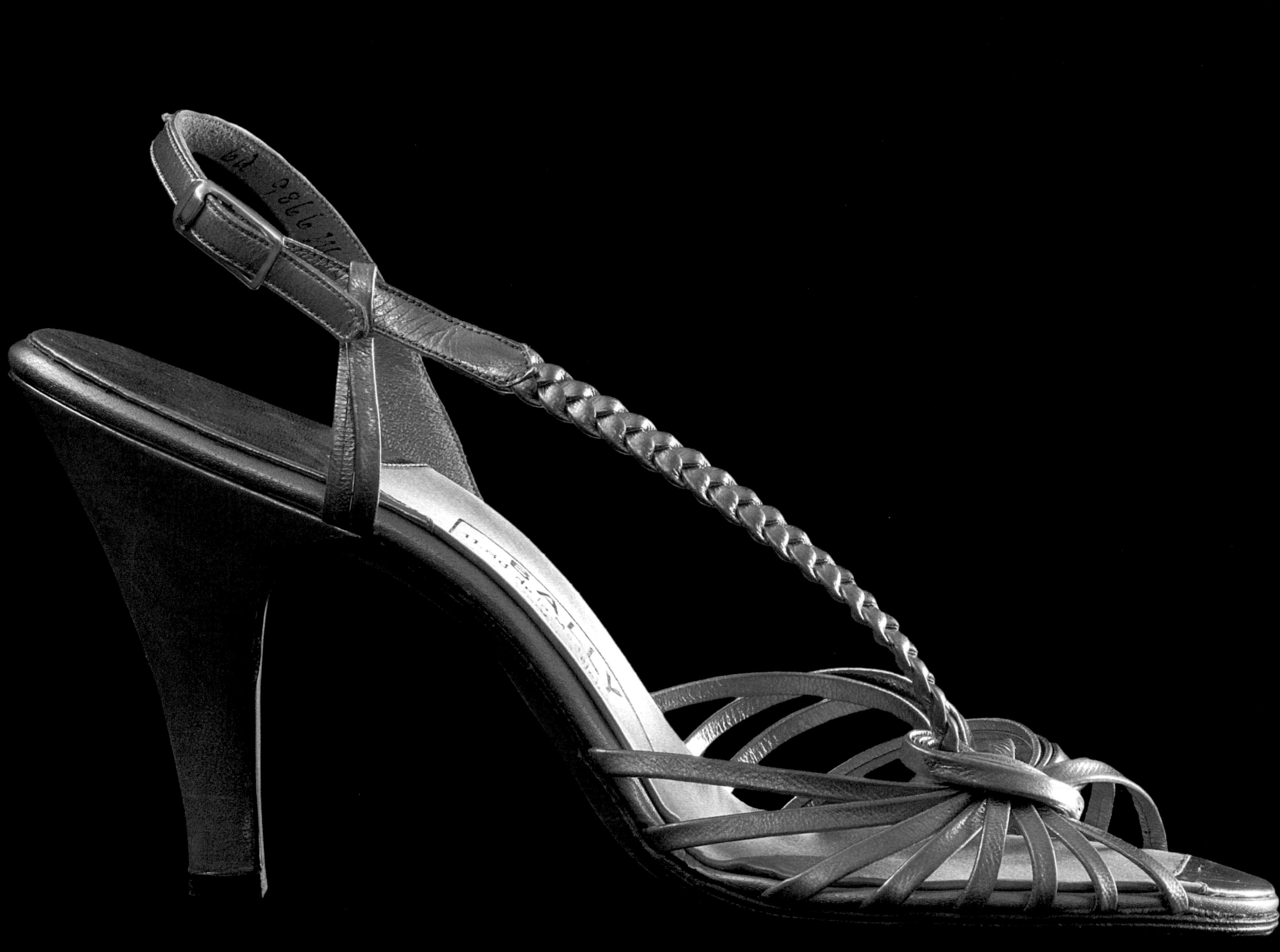

1955

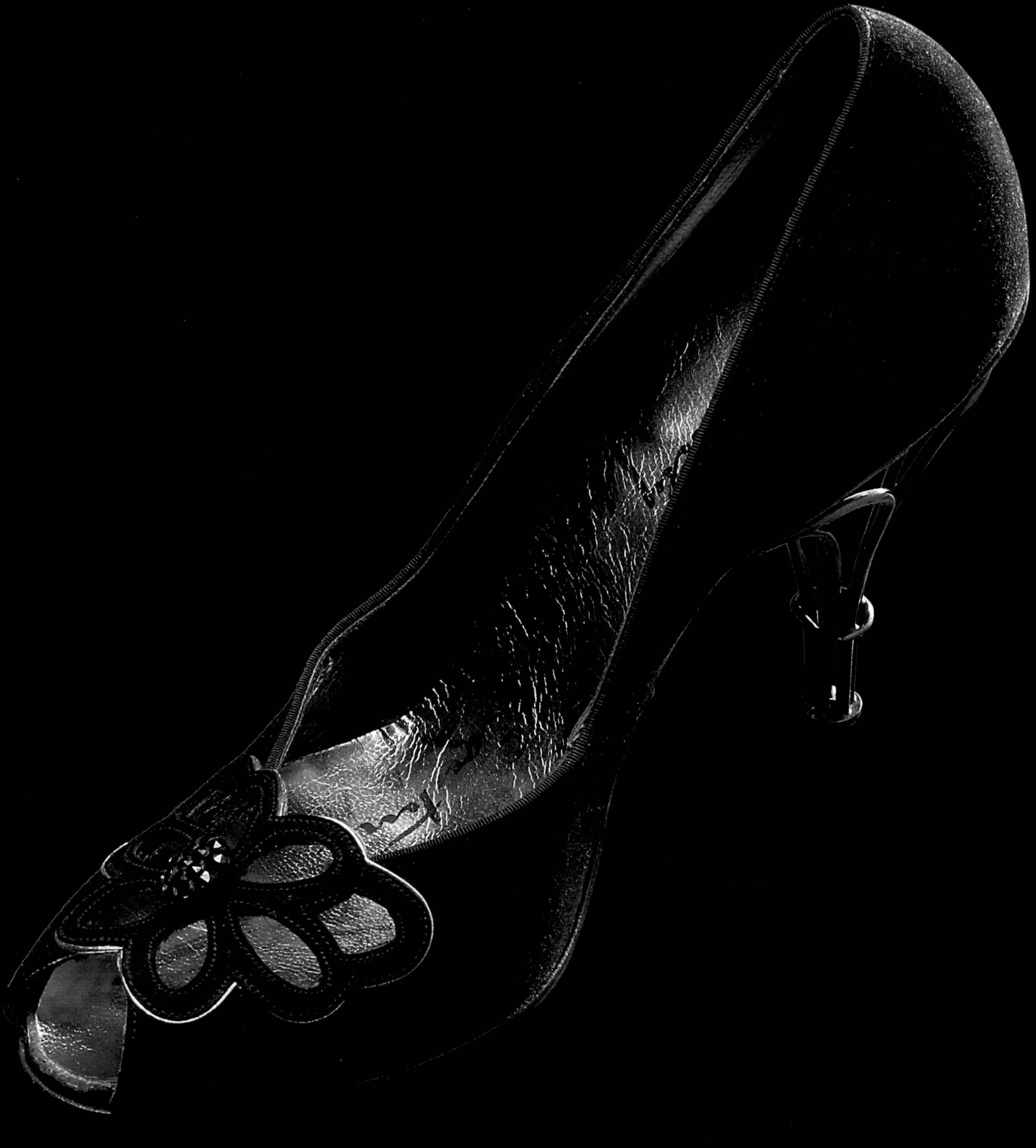

BALLY

Bernard Villemot, 1982

Chaussures „Bally"
MARQUE FAVORITE

Unknown, 1910

Bally

Ribas, 1924

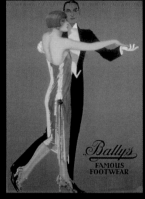

Bally's
FAMOUS
FOOTWEAR

Ribas, 1925

DŒLK
Chaussures „Bally"

Unknown, 1928

BALLY

Hans Aeschbach, 1943

BALLY

Bernard Villemot, 1990

Bally

Reynold Vuilleumier, 1937

Bally
CONFORT ELEGANCE QUALITE

Pierre Gauchat, 1936

BALLY
Miss

Franz Breitschmid, 1955

Eduard Stiefel, 1932

Ribas, 1926

Reynold Vuilleumier, 1937

Unknown, 1933

Franco Barberis, 1938

Pierre Augsburger, 1961

J. Demachy, 1949

Bernard Villemot, 1979

Theo Muvr, 1957

Franz Breitschmid, 1956

THE LIBRARY
WITHDRAWN
COLLEGE
SWINDON